WHEN SPRING COMES

Story and photographs

by

Charles Philip Fox

Reilly & Lee Co.
Chicago 1964

F

To Fred and Jolly Ott,
to whom the world of fields and forests
means so much.

TO TEACHERS AND PARENTS:

The beauty and vitality of the world around us are never more apparent than in spring. As the lengthening days breathe warmth onto the earth, flowers and trees begin to bud, birds come back from their wintering places, and animals emerge from hibernation. Nests are built, babies are born, and all of nature is filled with new life.

Spring is a time of intense activity in forests, fields, and marshes. Every plant and every animal is reproducing its kind in order to survive.

WHEN SPRING COMES is a companion book to WHEN WINTER COMES, which told how nature prepared for its long winter sleep. These new pictures show spring's awakening, full of loveliness and promise.

Charles Philip Fox
Oconomowoc, Wisconsin

Spring is here!

How can you tell?

Look!
The robins have come back.
There they are, three of them!
Snow is still on the ground.
But spring is here.
The robins know.
Soon leaves and flowers will be out.

Daffodils begin to grow.

Soon they are tall.

And now they have flowers!

See the many many dots in the sky? Those are birds. They
are coming back from the South, where they have been all
winter.

Mrs. Mallard Duck is on her nest.

When she leaves her nest she hides her eggs.

You cannot see them . . .

    unless you look very carefully.

Quick!
We will take a look at Mrs. Duck's eggs.
How many do you see?
Soon her babies will be hatched.

Mrs. Squirrel is moving into a new home.
Do you see where it will be?

Mrs. Squirrel's home is the hole in this hollow tree.
There is a warm nest inside.
Babies will be born here too.

Mrs. Duck's babies are out of their shells now.
Mrs. Squirrel watches them from her tree.

Mrs. Duck takes her babies down to the creek.
They would like to swim.
But she sees a hungry hawk.

Hawks eat baby birds . . .
if they can catch them!

Mrs. Duck hurries away.
The long grass will hide her babies.
They will be safe.

They hurry past a pine tree that
   has new little pine cones.
The pine cones look like little candles,
   but they are seeds. They will grow into
   new trees.

The maple tree has little buds.
Soon they will open into
new maple leaves.

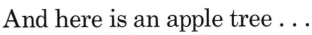

Here are new oak leaves.
They are little and soft and curly.

And here is an apple tree . . .

Spring is a time for flowers!

A baby deer comes out of the forest.
How warm the sun is!
He has white spots.
The spots help him hide in the long grass.
He eats the long grass too.

This little Flicker looks out.
He wants to eat something.

Here is Mother Flicker.
She feeds her baby.
There are four babies in her nest to feed.

The wood duck looks out of her home.
What does she see?

It is Mrs. Skunk . . .
And her new family of three little skunks.
They live under a stump when they are home.
They were born deep under the ground in a den.

Mr. Badger has made a deep hole.
His nest is of dry grass.
The Badger babies will be safe there.

Here comes Mrs. Opossum.
She takes her family with her.
And they all ride on her back!
How many little Opossums are there?

The robins have built a nest now.
It is made of mud and grass.

They have four blue eggs.

Here is a blackbird's nest.
Can you see it?
It is not in a tree.
It is in long grass.

Look!
In the nest are three blackbird eggs.

The baby robins come out of their shells.
Their mother has to work hard to feed them.

This is what robins eat.
We would not like it very much, I guess.
But robins find it very good.

And soon the baby robins will grow big and strong.

Can you see something?
There is something in the long grass.

It is a nest of baby rabbits.
Their mother has lined their nest with soft fur.

Now these babies are bigger.
And they come out to look around.

The little skunks are out walking . . .

The squirrel is in the tree . . .

The rabbits are warm and safe . . .

The opossums take a ride . . .

The deer is in the sun . . .   The little ducks are swimming . . .

when spring comes!

The robins are eating . . .   The flowers are blooming . . .